Finish Line
Comprehension Skills

H

Making Inferences

To the Student

Finish Line Comprehension Skills: Making Inferences is a practice series designed to provide additional practice in basic comprehension skills and strategies. In Part I, each major skill is presented through a teaching lesson that explains it and walks you through a sample question and answer. Part II refers you to the introductory pages in Part I for help and then gives you many examples for practice.

This book contains folktales and other fiction passages, poetry, and many nonfiction articles. The articles tell about real-life adventures, famous people, interesting places, and important events. There are questions after each passage that help you identify inferences and conclusions. These questions are similar to those found on most standardized tests. You can become a better reader and test-taker as you go through this book and focus on understanding.

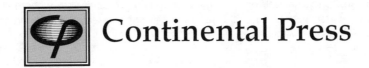

Continental Press

Acknowledgments

Pages 4, 7, 8, 14, 17, 25, 30, 39 Margaret Lindmark; Page 24 www.en.wikipedia.org

ISBN 978-0-8454-3921-0

Table of Contents

PART I
Making Inferences

A writer does not state every fact plainly. Whether you're reading nonfiction or fiction, the writer assumes that you can figure out some details by combining what you're reading with your prior knowledge and experience—what you already know. This is called **making inferences.**

Read the passage. Then answer the question that follows.

"Part of your job will be closing up at night," Ms. Cho said. "Shut down the grill at 11. Clean it well with this soap and brush. Then clean the milkshake machine. Save the coffee machine for last. Throw out the last of the grounds. Run plain hot water through the machine and then wash each part by hand. Make absolutely sure you turn off the deep fryer, but don't worry about cleaning it. Theresa takes care of that when she opens up in the morning." Cliff nodded. He hoped he would remember all those details without having to ask Ms. Cho to repeat any.

This paragraph is about Cliff's new job at a—

A   laundry

B   bookstore

C   restaurant

D   auto-repair shop

Making Inferences

The paragraph doesn't say where this story is taking place. But Ms. Cho's detailed instructions include a grill, milkshake machine, and deep fryer. You know that these items are all used in a restaurant—choice C.

What you read:	What you know:	Inference:
• Cliff must clean a grill and milkshake machine and turn off the deep fryer.	• These items are found in the kitchen of a restaurant.	• Cliff is working in a restaurant.

Drawing Conclusions

Writers may also give you pieces of information that you can put together to determine other facts. When you do that, you are **drawing conclusions** or **making generalizations**.

Read the passage. Then answer the question that follows.

The electric eel is not a true eel. But, like true eels, it is a fish with a long, tube-shaped body. It is a freshwater fish, native to South American rivers, and can grow to be eight feet long. In its tail is an organ that acts like a battery. The eel uses it to stun or to kill its prey and also to keep predators away. It also uses its electricity to find its way in the water. It sends out pulses of electricity that bounce off objects and return to it, much as a bat uses sound waves. The eel can sense animals and objects blocking its path and move safely around them.

You can conclude from this passage that—

A   an electric eel's electricity can power a flashlight

B   electricity is a useful tool for the electric eel

C   electric eels cannot harm human beings

D   people cannot safely eat electric eels

Drawing Conclusions

What conclusion can you draw from the information in the passage? The electric eel's electricity is strong enough to kill a fish, so you can't conclude that it cannot harm people as well. Its electric organ may act like a battery, but you can't conclude that people can use it *as* a battery. (Would it work if the eel is dead?) Nor can you conclude that it isn't edible, like other dangerous fish. But you can conclude that the eel's electricity is a useful tool for survival—choice B.

On this proof chart, write <u>two</u> more details that support the conclusion that electricity is a useful tool for the electric eel.

Conclusion	Proof
For electric eels, electricity is a useful tool.	1. Electric eels use electricity to keep enemies away. 2. _____ _____ 3. _____ _____

Predicting Outcomes

As you read, you often think ahead to what will happen next. Doing this helps move the passage along in your mind. When you are **predicting outcomes,** you are making inferences based on information in the selection and your prior knowledge, or drawing conclusions from the details in the selection.

Read the passage. Then answer the question that follows.

Josh Was Curious

We used to call my brother Josh "Curious George" when he was little. He especially wanted to know how things worked. From the time he was two, he was always taking things apart—toys, clocks, telephones, pencil sharpeners. Of course, he wasn't so good at putting them back together. Between my parents' rules and our making sure to keep dangerous things out of Josh's reach, we were mostly able to avoid disaster. Then came the summer day when Josh wanted to know what made the toilet bowl refill with water after he flushed it.

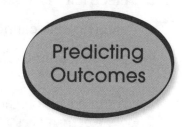

If this were the first paragraph of a story, you could predict that it would be—

A   a story about how Josh's curiosity put the family in danger

B   a story about how Josh grew up to be a famous inventor

C   a story about how Josh fixed the family's plumbing

D   a funny story

You know something about stories because you've read a lot of them. The last sentence of the paragraph suggests what the story will be about. It will likely end with little Josh very proud of his discovery but still a small child. There will be a big mess to clean up, but no one in danger. Choice D is correct.

What happens	What will happen
A child wants to know how things work. He becomes curious about the toilet bowl. The author takes a humorous tone.	something funny involving plumbing—perhaps a flood of water in the house

The first paragraphs of an article or story often give you an idea of what to expect. A title or illustration may also be a clue. Some types of stories guide you in predicting what will happen. The tortoise will beat the hare. Something scary will happen in an old house. The wise peasant girl will outwit the king—or marry him. And sometimes you have to change your predictions as you read further.

Finish Line Comprehension Skills

Inferring Word Meaning

Often when you read, you come across words you don't know. You can keep a dictionary by your side and look up the meaning of an unfamiliar word. But often you can **infer the meaning from context clues.** To find the meaning of an unknown word, look at how it is used in the sentence and in the whole passage. Look for clues that will help you guess the meaning. Synonyms, antonyms, examples, and descriptions may be context clues. Sometimes a definition may even be given somewhere in the passage.

Read the passage. Then answer the questions that follow.

Having played four games in four *consecutive* nights, the team was tired. Playing all those games without a day to rest might be OK for a baseball team, but basketball players are in constant motion. Because they were so *fatigued*, they were dropping passes and missing easy shots. It was almost as though they were asleep on their feet.

As used in the passage, the word *consecutive* means—

A following one right after the other

B with growing excitement

C at rest

D exact

Inferring Word Meaning

You can tell what *consecutive* means from the sentence that follows. The team played those four games without a day to rest. You can infer that the team played on four nights in a row. The correct answer is choice A.

As used in the passage, the word *fatigued* means—

A tired   **B** angry   **C** foolish   **D** excited

The context of both the sentence and the paragraph points you to the correct answer—choice A. The sentence tells you that because the players were fatigued, they were dropping passes and missing easy shots. The paragraph tells you that they had played four nights in a row and were almost "asleep on their feet." You can infer from these clues that *fatigued* means "tired."

© The Continental Press, Inc.   Do not duplicate.

Determining Cause-and-Effect Relationships

People are curious creatures who want to know why things happen. So it's important to understand causes. Authors will often explain causes by using words like *because, so, in order that,* or *as a result.* But sometimes you have to make an inference to determine the cause-and-effect relationship. The thing that happens is the **effect.** What makes it happen, or the reason it happens, is the **cause.**

Read the passage. Then answer the questions that follow.

No one knows for certain how long people have used skis. But skis that are nearly 5,000 years old have been found in Sweden and Finland. Did skiers that long ago have races and jumping competitions? Well, maybe. But fun was not the main reason that people used skis. Sweden and Finland are in a snowy part of the world, and skis make it easier to move on snow. On those early cross-country skis, a person could go more than 30 miles an hour. There would be no faster way to travel until railroads came along. People used skis to move heavy loads, which they dragged behind them on a kind of sled. They even hunted on skis, carrying bows and arrows on their backs.

Based on the paragraph, what is the *main* reason people first used skis?

Cause-and-Effect
Relationships

_____

_____

The paragraph doesn't say directly why skis were invented. But the content suggests the reason—transportation in the snow. People on skis could move over 30 miles an hour and move heavy loads. That made skis a most practical invention.

Why would humans have found it especially useful to hunt on skis?

_____

_____

To answer this question, you have to make an inference based on what you know about hunting and about snow. You know that some people such as early Native Americans hunted by following the tracks of animals. You know that tracks are easy to follow in the snow. If you have a way to follow animal tracks by moving rapidly through the snow, your family will be well fed during the winter.

Inferring Story Elements

When you read a story, you are frequently **making inferences about story elements,** the setting and characters, as you did in the paragraph on page 4 about the young man starting a job at a restaurant. An author of fiction often lets a character's thoughts and actions speak for themselves. It's up to you to infer from those thoughts and actions whether a character is brave, foolish, careful, impatient, or any other of the wide variety of human characteristics. In a traditional tale, such as this Aesop fable, you may also infer the lesson the story teaches.

The Donkey and His Masters

A donkey belonged to a vegetable peddler who fed him little and made him carry heavy sacks. The donkey asked Zeus, the king of the gods, to free him from this service and find him a different master. Soon afterward, he got his wish and was sold to a brick maker. But this master made him carry even heavier loads and fed him no better than he was before. So the donkey again petitioned Zeus for a change of master. The god, warning him that this was the last time he would honor the donkey's request, commanded that he be sold to a tanner. This man could find no use for the donkey except to turn his hide into leather.

Which word would *best* describe the donkey in this story?

A lazy

C stubborn

B lucky

D discontented

Most characters in fiction, like real people, are a complex combination of character traits. But in a simple tale like this, one word is usually enough to describe a character, human or otherwise. The donkey keeps ending up with worse masters because he is always complaining about the one he has. The word that best describes him is discontented—choice D.

What is the lesson this story teaches?

_____

_____

A question like this has no single correct answer. One possible answer is, "A person who grumbles in one situation is likely to grumble in any situation." Can you think of others?

Read each selection. Then answer the questions about making inferences.

Stay away from hippos. The hippopotamus, though a plant eater, kills more humans than any other mammal in Africa. Just ask safari guide Paul Templer. An angry hippo went after Templer after smashing into his canoe. Templer slid into his wide-open mouth. The animal chewed into Templer's back, shook him, then spit him out. Templer swam for shore, but the hippo grabbed him by the legs and pulled him under. Kicking and clawing, Templer tried to break free. When the hippo finally let him go, he struggled to the surface and started swimming again. Then the hippo attacked for the third time. It bit into Templer's side before finally leaving him alone. Templer was rushed to the hospital. Though doctors had to *amputate* his left arm, Templer was lucky. Few people who are attacked by a hippopotamus live to tell the tale.

1 What is the *most likely* reason the hippo attacked Templer?

A It was hungry.

B Templer had tried to shoot it.

C It felt threatened by a human presence.

D It thought Templer's boat was a crocodile.

Cause-and-Effect Relationships

PAGE 8

2 When the hippo attacked Templer for the third time, he *probably* felt—

A brave   **B** angry   **C** surprised   **D** terrified

3 The hippopotamus kills more humans than any other mammal in Africa. Which of the following is *not* an African mammal?

A lion   **B** python   **C** elephant   **D** chimpanzee

4 How did Templer *most likely* feel when he left the hospital?

A sad but relieved   **C** worried and upset

B angry but excited   **D** eager to return to work

Finish Line Comprehension Skills

5 In this selection, the word *amputate* means—

A find

B cut off

C weaken

D experiment on

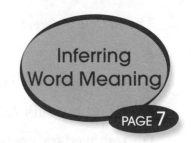

Inferring
Word Meaning

PAGE 7

Komodo Island is part of the large island nation of Indonesia, in Southeast Asia. It is a national park and a World Heritage Site. The Komodo dragon, at 300 pounds the world's largest lizard, makes its home there. About a thousand of these carnivores live on Komodo, which is also home to more poisonous snakes and spiders than any other place its size. To top it off, the waters around Komodo Island are filled with sharks.

1 You can conclude from this selection that Komodo Island—

A is rarely visited by people

B can be a dangerous place

C is good for farming

D gets little rainfall

2 You can infer that Komodo Island was made a national park mainly because of its—

A wildlife   B hiking trails   C historic sites   D natural beauty

---

Scientists have recognized and named about 1.5 million animal species, and they're not done yet. Since 2005, more than 50 new species have been discovered on Borneo, an island of Southeast Asia. They include a tree-dwelling kangaroo. And in 2007, an expedition to the *remote* highlands of Suriname, in South America, turned up 24 new species. What was unusual about the Suriname discovery was that many of the new species were not insects. They included six species of fish and four new frogs, including a dark-purple one with glowing light-purple markings. The scientists of Conservation International, which sponsored the expedition, hope that the government of Suriname will protect the unexplored area from mining activity.

1 In this article, a "new" species means one that—

A has never been seen by human beings before

B has never been described by science before

C only recently appeared on Earth

D is new to a particular region

2 The article suggests that *most* newly discovered animals are—

A insects

B endangered species

C found in South America

D removed for preservation in zoos

3 In this article, the word *remote* means—

A controlled at a distance

B hard to reach

C desert-like

D unfriendly

The cotton-top tamarin lives in the treetops in the rain forest of northwest Colombia. It stands only nine inches high and weighs about one pound. Its tail is longer than its body, but unlike many related species, it doesn't use its tail for locomotion. Instead it moves by climbing, scampering along branches, and leaping from branch to branch. It eats mostly fruit, leaves, and plant juices, but also insects and other small animals such as lizards.

Cotton-top tamarins travel in groups of up to 15. The groups are made up of two adult parents, their young, and unrelated "helpers." The group shares food and the care of the young. The parents take on the most responsibility, and male and female share their duties evenly. By helping their parents care for the youngest members of the group, older brothers and sisters learn how to raise their own young.

1 The cotton-top tamarin is—

A a squirrel-like animal

B a very small monkey

C a flightless bird

D a great ape

2 Cotton-top tamarins are aided in survival by—

A using their tails to escape predators

B feeding in the tops of trees

C living in family groups

D ferocity in hunting

3 Use this chart to show evidence for your conclusion. Write your answers to questions 1 and 2 under **Conclusion.** Then, under **Proof,** write three details that back up each conclusion.

Drawing Conclusions

Conclusion	Proof
1.	1. _____ _____ 2. _____ _____ 3. _____ _____
2.	1. _____ _____ 2. _____ _____ 3. _____ _____

Making Inferences

© The Continental Press, Inc.   Do not duplicate.

The Peasant and the King

Tobias, an elderly peasant, was finishing his farm chores one day when he heard the joyful sound of hunting horns and the baying of hounds. He looked up to see the king and his nobles riding back from their day's hunting.

The king motioned to three of his ministers to attend him. Then to Tobias's amazement, the royal party rode up to him. Tobias took off his cap and bowed deeply.

"Greetings, old man," said the king. "Did you not rise early enough to do your work?"

"I did, Sire," replied Tobias, "but the Good Lord did not allow me."

The king then asked, "Grandfather, how long has the snowy orchard been blooming on yonder sage mountaintop?"

"Forty years already, Your Majesty."

Nodding his head gravely, the king asked, "How long have those streams been flowing from under the mountain?"

"For more than fifteen years, Sire, they have been flowing freely," answered Tobias.

"So far, so good," said the king. "Now, when three foolish geese from the South come to you, will you be ready to fleece them?"

"Oh, very well indeed, Your Majesty," the old man replied without hesitation.

Smiling, the king gave the old peasant his golden hunt cup and rode home with his ministers to the palace.

After dinner that evening, the king asked his three ministers to explain his questions to old Tobias and the peasant's responses. The ministers thought hard, making wild and improbable guesses. Finally he grew impatient and told them they had thirty days to find the answers or lose their positions.

Failing to come up with answers to the riddles, the three ministers went to the old peasant themselves. They begged; they pleaded; they threatened. Tobias stood fast and refused to enlighten them. Desperate, each minister placed one hundred pieces of gold on the table. Only then did Tobias reveal the meaning of the riddles.

"My first answer to our beloved king meant that I had married young and had children, but that the Good Lord took them from me. The second answer explained that forty years ago, my hair turned white. Then the king asked how long the streams had been flowing, meaning my tears of grief."

"Finally, you are the three foolish geese from the South, my lord, who came to pay for my explanation. And as I promised the king, the geese have been well fleeced!"

Finish Line Comprehension Skills

1 What was the king's probable reason for his actions?

    A He wanted Tobias to become one of his ministers.

    B He wanted to test his ministers to see how clever they were.

    C He thought the ministers could learn about farming from Tobias.

    D He wanted to punish his ministers for being better hunters than he was.

Making Inferences

PAGE **4**

2 How can you tell that the king was speaking in riddles to Tobias?

_____

_____

_____

3 When Tobias explained to the ministers "the Good Lord took [his children]," he meant that—

    A the Lord sent them away to seek their fortune

    B they took vows and entered a monastery

    C they went on a religious pilgrimage

    D they all died

4 In the last paragraph, the word _fleeced_ means—

    A made to look foolish

    B robbed of their clothing

    C given what they came for

    D tricked out of their money

The *Titanic* was declared by its owner to be an unsinkable ship. But on the night of April 14, 1912, it struck an iceberg and sank to the bottom of the North Atlantic. More than 1,500 lives were lost. For decades the public was fascinated by this tragic disaster. It was the subject of books, movies, and plays. People often spoke of locating the wreck, but it seemed an impossible task.

In the 1970s, a young scientist named Robert Ballard was helping the U.S. Navy to build small, unmanned *submersibles*— underwater vessels used for exploring the deep ocean. They were outfitted with lights, cameras and robot arms and controlled by a ship at the surface. Ballard realized that this could be a way of locating the *Titanic*.

Ballard's first attempt, in 1977, ended in failure when costly search equipment fell into the sea. But in 1985, he tried again. This time he brought a submersible called *Argo* that he had designed himself. It had two TV-camera eyes that could show pictures as the vessel traveled over the sea bottom 12,500 feet below.

Ballard's team took turns watching the TV monitors. For weeks all they showed were *monotonous* pictures of mud, with the occasional deep-sea creature. But early on the morning of September 1, 1985, Ballard's team saw small holes, like impact craters. Soon afterward they spotted debris. Finally a round shape appeared. Ballard recognized it as a boiler from one of the *Titanic's* engines. Soon afterward, the hull was located. A year later, Ballard would return to study the wreck in detail. Meanwhile, he and his crew had some celebrating to do.

1 How did Ballard *probably* feel when he spotted the boiler?

A shocked

B nervous

C excited

D confident

Inferring Story Elements

PAGE 9

2 In paragraph 4, what does the word *monotonous* mean?

A unchanging   **B** interesting   **C** puzzling   **D** invisible

3 Ballard *probably* recognized the boiler because—

A it had the name *Titanic* on it

B it looked like modern ships' boilers

C it was the biggest piece of the *Titanic*

D he had studied pictures of the *Titanic*

Finish Line Comprehension Skills

Plum Blossoms

by Buson

Does it float upward,

The scent of the plum-blossoms?

Halo 'round the moon

1 This type of poem, a haiku, comes from—

A Japan

B England

C Mexico

D North Africa

2 What is the speaker saying in this poem?

_____

_____

_____

_____

Mount Vesuvius is a volcano in Italy. It has erupted many times, but its most famous outburst took place during the time of the Roman Empire, on August 24, A.D. 79. Hot ash, molten rock, and poisonous gases poured down on the city of Pompeii, a resort town popular among Rome's wealthy classes. Most of the city's 20,000 people managed to escape. Those who remained behind—perhaps 2,000 in all—were buried under 13 feet of ash and rock. And so was Pompeii.

As the centuries passed, Pompeii was nearly forgotten. It was accidentally rediscovered twice, in 1599 and 1748, but it was not until 1860 that archaeologists began the work of _systematically_ digging it out. Today much of Pompeii looks almost exactly the same as it did before the great eruption. Visitors walk through its homes and shops and view perfectly preserved artwork, street signs, and even graffiti. For historians, Pompeii is a window into the everyday life of the Roman Empire.

1 In paragraph 2, what does the word *systematically* mean?

   A secretly

   B eagerly

   C at great cost

   D in an organized way

2 What is the *most likely* reason that most people in Pompeii were able to escape the eruption?

   A The volcano had been rumbling for several days.

   B Volcano scientists warned them to get out.

   C Fortune tellers had predicted the eruption.

   D They were only vacationing there.

3 Why does Pompeii look almost the same today as it did in A.D. 79?

_____

_____

4 How does Pompeii help historians understand the past?

_____

_____

_____

_____

It was once a common scene in action movies and TV shows: a character steps into quicksand and begins to sink. The more she struggles, the faster she goes under. Just as she is about to vanish, the hero extends a branch and drags her to safety.

There is some exaggeration to the scene, but also some truth. Quicksand is actually a mixture of water with finely grained earth, clay, and salt. It appears solid, but it acts like a liquid when someone steps into it. Pressure causes some of the liquid and solid contents to separate. This makes other parts of the mixture more dense, so more force is needed to push through it. The best thing to do if you find yourself in quicksand is to lie on your back. Spread your arms and legs, as if you're floating in a swimming pool, and you'll stop sinking. Slowly drift to solid ground and pull yourself out.

1 According to the article, who is *most likely* to escape after walking into quicksand?

   A a calm person

   B a strong person

   C a good swimmer

   D a person with a friend nearby

Finish Line Comprehension Skills

2 Which is the *main* reason that people sink in quicksand?

A It contains clay.

B They can't swim.

C It sucks people in.

D It is largely liquid.

May Chinn was a high-school dropout. She quit school because of poverty and "heartache over a lost boyfriend." This was the way she told the story years later, when she was a famous doctor.

May's father had been born a slave on a Virginia plantation but had escaped at the age of 11. Her mother was a Native American of the Chickahominy people. Lulu Ann Chinn had a dream that her daughter would get an education. To earn money for that goal, she worked two jobs. One was as a cook for the wealthy Tiffany family. The Tiffanys treated young May as a member of the family. They taught her to speak several languages and took her to concerts in New York. That was where she heard "classical" music for the first time. She *subsequently* became a fine piano player herself. She worked occasional jobs as a musician in concerts and in churches, and would play the piano all her life.

In 1917, a friend of May's received a scholarship to Columbia University. May was 21 and had been out of school for several years, but she decided to take the entrance exams herself. To her surprise, she was accepted. At first she planned to study music. But a teacher insulted her, saying that African Americans were not suited for

classical music. At about the same time, another teacher praised a paper she had written for a health class and encouraged her to study science. By her senior year, May was working in a medical laboratory. In 1926, she graduated from medical school. She worked as a family doctor and a cancer specialist at New York hospitals. She often went into dangerous neighborhoods to treat people who would not otherwise have seen a doctor. Late in her life, she formed a committee to help African American women go to medical school. She practiced medicine until she was 81, three years before her death.

1 To build a career in medicine, May Chinn *most likely* had to—

A overcome people's prejudices

B earn money as a musician

C keep returning to school

D pay back many debts

Making Inferences

2 The article portrays May Chinn as a person who—

   A helped others

   B was easily discouraged

   C was driven to make money

   D had trouble making up her mind

3 In paragraph 2, the word *subsequently* means—

   A at the beginning   **B** surprisingly   **C** sometimes   **D** later

4 Looking back on her life, May Chinn had several people to feel thankful for. Describe how *three* people helped her in her early years.

_____

_____

_____

_____

The planet Venus has sometimes been called Earth's twin. It is only slightly smaller than our planet. It is the next planet closer to the sun. But Venus is covered with a thick layer of clouds. Little was actually known about the planet until space probes reached it during the 1960s. Venus's atmosphere is mostly made up of carbon dioxide. This blanket of "greenhouse gas" traps the sun's heat so that it cannot escape. The planet's average temperature is about 800 degrees Fahrenheit, hot enough to melt lead. Venus probably once had water like Earth, but it is now quite dry. The pressure of the atmosphere at the surface is about 90 times greater than Earth's. The cloud layers are largely made up of sulfuric acid, which can dissolve metal. Earth and Venus may appear to be twins from far away, but up close it's a different story.

1 Why is there no longer any water on Venus?

_____

_____

2 What *probably* happened to the first space probes that landed on Venus?

_____

_____

3 Use this chart to show how you inferred your answers to questions 1 and 2.

What you read:	What you know:	Inference:
1. _____ _____ _____ _____	1. _____ _____ _____ _____	1. _____ _____ _____ _____
2. _____ _____ _____ _____	2. _____ _____ _____ _____	2. _____ _____ _____ _____

Between 1969 and 1972, twelve American astronauts walked on the moon. All these moon walkers left footprints behind. On Earth these prints would have been long gone by now, but they all remain on the moon to this day. There is no wind on the moon to blow them away. There is no rain to wash them away. But the footprints won't last forever. Bits of rock called meteorites frequently hit the moon. Little by little, over thousands or perhaps millions of years, they will *erode* the footprints.

1 The article suggests that footprints in remote areas on Earth do *not* last long because of—

  A weather

  B meteorites

  C animal movements

  D human activity

2 The word *erode* in this article means to—

  A preserve

  B wear away

  C make invisible

  D make people forget

Making Inferences

SPRING BAND SPECTACULAR!
Riverside Middle School Marching Band

The award-winning Riverside Middle School Marching Band has been invited to march in the annual Thanksgiving Day Parade in New York City, on November 27. This is a great honor for our school, since only the best bands in the country are chosen, and...

WE WERE ONE OF THE LUCKY ONES!

In order to make the trip east, the Riverside Marching Band needs $3,000 for transportation and room and board. To help us raise those funds, we're planning a series of band concerts and other activities throughout the spring. Here's our

SCHEDULE OF IMPORTANT EVENTS!

SWING INTO SPRING

Riverside Marching Band in Concert
When: March 21, 22, 24, and 26
Where: Clampett Auditorium
Tickets: Adults $5.00, Children $3.50

EAT HEARTY

Riverside Marching Band Bake Sale
When: April 1 and 15
Where: Riverside Middle School gym
All donations gratefully accepted!

MAY FLOWERS CAR WASH

When: every Saturday & Sunday in May
Where: Tony's Service Station, at the corner of Second and Elm
How much: $5/car, $8/truck or van

FAREWELL TO GRADS

Sing Along with the Band and Chorus!
Friday, June 6, and Saturday, June 7
7:30 P.M. at Park & Rec Baseball Field
Tickets: Adults $7.00, Children $4.00

<u>Special Sponsors:</u> If you want your personal or business name listed in our concert programs, please call Mr. Brian Godfrey, our music director, at 555-5393. If you would like to donate your time or a gift of money, he would be happy to give you any other information you might need.

PLEASE HELP TO MAKE OUR CHANCE OF A LIFETIME A REALITY!

1 The people who wrote this notice were *probably*—

A nervous and scared

B thrilled and defiant

C excited and honored

D frustrated and angry

2 What can you assume about the students in the band?

A They don't want to march in the parade because of the extra practicing involved.

B They are willing to work hard for the money they need to make the trip.

C They are doubtful about being able to earn enough money for the trip.

D They are unwilling to give up their spare time to raise money.

3 Besides the events listed in the notice, how else are the students trying to raise money?

A by auctioning off old instruments

B by starting a student-owned business

C through a loan from Mr. Godfrey, their music director

D from advertisements in their concert programs and donations of money

4 If the $3,000 is not raised by June, the band members will *probably*—

A march in a parade closer to home

B not be able to march in the parade

C plan more fund-raising events for the fall

D send only half the band to New York City

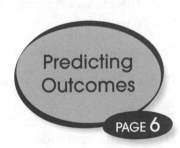

Predicting Outcomes

PAGE 6

How did a missed nap lead to the world's most famous drugstore? Ted Hustead and his family operated a drugstore in the town of Wall, South Dakota. In 1936, business was bad. It looked as though the store would have to close. One sizzling summer afternoon, Ted's wife, Dorothy, felt tired and went home to take a nap. But trucks on the highway were making so much noise that she couldn't sleep. Thoughts of all those people *sweltering* in their cars and trucks gave her an idea: Why not put up a sign offering a free glass of ice water to anyone who stopped at Wall Drug Store?

As soon as Dorothy put up her sign, cars started pulling off the highway. Before long, the Husteads had to enlarge the store to allow for all the customers. So they put up more signs along South Dakota's highways and in other states, too. Word got around that Wall Drug Store was the place to go. During World War II, homesick American soldiers fighting in distant lands put up signs saying how far it was to Wall Drug Store.

Since then, signs such as "6,383 miles to Wall Drug" have appeared on London buses, on the Paris subway, and at the Taj Mahal in India, as well as all over the United States. Today the store is run by the Husteads' grandchildren. It employs nearly one-third of the town's residents. Oh, and every visitor—20,000 on a good summer day—still gets a free glass of ice water.

1 The success of Wall Drug Store is *mainly* due to—

   A low prices

   B special sales

   C signs in distant places

   D Dorothy Hustead's idea

2 Dorothy Hustead guessed that people who stopped for free ice water would—

   A see something they wanted to buy

   B tell their friends about the store

   C take home a free sign

   D use the restrooms

3 In paragraph 1, the word *sweltering* means—

   A going fast

   B making noise

   C hungry and thirsty

   D suffering from heat

Finish Line Comprehension Skills

When I Heard the Learn'd Astronomer

by Walt Whitman

When I heard the learn'd astronomer,
When the proofs, the figures, were ranged in columns before me,
When I was shown the charts and diagrams, to add, divide, and
    measure them,
When I sitting heard the astronomer where he lectured with
    much applause in the lecture-room,
How soon unaccountable I became tired and sick,
Till rising and gliding out I wander'd off by myself,
In the mystical moist night-air and from time to time,
Look'd up in perfect silence at the stars.

1 What point is the poet making in this poem? Explain your
answer and why you agree or disagree with his point.

_____

_____

_____

In many parts of the world, family names were once only for nobles and the very rich. Ordinary people had only a personal name. But in many towns or villages there would be several people who had the same name. People needed a way to distinguish which Will or Mary they were talking about. Some were known by the name of a parent, such as Will, Robin's Son. Others might be known by their occupation, such as Joe Baker or Joe Tailor. Still others might be known by a distinguishing physical characteristic or personality trait. That's Jane Short's house, while Red-headed Jane lives over there. Others were named for where they lived, such as John Woods or John-by-the Rockslide. Someone else might be known by the place where he or she used to live. A famous example is the great artist and scientist, Leonardo da Vinci, whose life overlapped the 15th and 16th centuries. As "a man of no family," his name was simply "Leonardo." The *da Vinci* part indicated that he came from a town called Vinci. It was not a family name.

Then governments (usually kings) began demanding that people take last names, the better to control them. This happened at different times in different countries. Many people simply took the name they were known by. The difference was that now they passed this name on to their children. John Woods's children (and their children) were now called Woods even if they lived far from a forest. And the family of "Jack, Will's Son" were called "the Wilsons" many generations after that original Will was dead.

1 Why didn't people need last names many years ago?

_____

_____

2 A person known as "Elizabeth Rivers" was *probably* called that because of—

   A her occupation

   B where she lived

   C what she looked like

   D the name of her father

3 A family named Truman *probably* had an ancestor who was noted for his—

   A honesty   **B** strength   **C** large ears   **D** sense of humor

4 If Leonardo da Vinci had had children—

   A they would have had the last name "Artist"

   B they would have been called "Leonardoson"

   C they would not have had the name "da Vinci"

   D they would probably have been famous in their time

5 What were some specific reasons that governments would have wanted people to have family names?

_____

_____

A plane out of Seattle was an hour behind schedule when it took off for Chicago. But it arrived only ten minutes late. Fortunately for the passengers, a jet stream rushed the plane to Chicago's O'Hare Airport.

No one knew about jet streams until the 1940s. They are encountered only at about 30,000 feet and higher. Pilots noticed that when they flew from west to east, they seemed to arrive at their *destination* earlier than expected. When they flew east to west, their flights took longer.

Jet streams are rivers of air high in the sky that are powerful enough to push a plane or to hold it back a bit. They usually flow from west to east. In summer, a jet stream may move along at 100 miles per hour. But in winter, they may reach three times that speed.

1 Which of these planes will *probably* move fastest?

   A a plane flying from California to New York in summer

   B a plane flying from New York to California in summer

   C a plane flying from California to New York in winter

   D a plane flying from New York to California in winter

Finish Line Comprehension Skills

2 Why were jet streams *not* discovered until the 1940s?

   A Early planes were too slow.

   B Pilots were not as well trained.

   C Early planes did not fly high enough.

   D Early planes' instruments were not accurate

3 In paragraph 2, the word *destination* refers to—

   A the place where a plane is going

   B the top speed achieved by a plane

   C the place where a plane started

   D the maximum height reached by a plane

Alexander Graham Bell was a teacher of the deaf. He invented the telephone while experimenting with ways to help the hearing impaired. The telephone, in turn, led to the invention of the battery-powered hearing aid. Like the telephone, the hearing aid changes sounds into electrical signals. An amplifier makes the signals stronger. A receiver then changes the signal back into a louder sound.

The first hearing aids were large, clumsy, and hard to use. Today's models are much smaller. They can also be adjusted in a number of ways to make sounds easier to hear and understand. Hearing aids that are built into eyeglasses have been around for 50 years. Digital hearing aids that use a tiny computer chip can be programmed for different situations, such as listening to music or being in a noisy crowd. The user looks like she is wearing a stylish wireless headset.

1 The article suggests that the invention of the telephone—

   A was a lucky accident

   B was intended to aid the deaf

   C was achieved by a deaf person

   D made use of hearing-aid batteries

2 Which conclusion can you draw from the article?

   A Hearing aids built into eyeglasses are the most expensive kind.

   B Over the years, hearing aids have improved.

   C The first hearing aids looked like telephones.

   D Smaller hearing aids produce weaker signals.

3 Use this chart to show evidence for your conclusion. Write your answer to question 2 under **Conclusion.** Then, under **Proof,** write three details that back up your conclusion.

Conclusion	Proof
	1. _____ _____ 2. _____ _____ 3. _____ _____

Olives picked and eaten right from the tree have a bitter flavor. The unpleasant taste is produced by a chemical called oleuropein, found only in olives. No one knows how people learned that olives can actually be made good to eat, but it must have happened more than 3,500 years ago. Somehow they discovered that treating them with lye and salt water changes their bitterness to a rich, pleasing flavor. The treatment could be risky, however. Lye is a burning chemical called an alkali. Until people got the process right, the lye undoubtedly poisoned more people than the bitter olives did.

Olives are soaked in a solution that is only one to two percent lye. The rest is water. The lye combines with the bitter-tasting oleuropein to produce a new chemical that is neither lye or oleuropein. The olives are kept in this alkali bath until the chemical seeps through to the hard pits at their center. This process may take three days. An expert keeps testing the olives to see if they're ready. This job can be dangerous because of the burning lye. As soon as the process is complete, the olives are removed from the lye solution. They are then rinsed thoroughly in water. This step takes about a week. Finally, they are *submerged* in salt water to bring out the delicious olive taste.

1 You can assume that the lye is *mainly* used to—

A give the olives a salty taste

B produce the delicious olive taste

C burn away the pits from the olives

D remove oleuropein from the olives

Finish Line Comprehension Skills

2 This passage would *most likely* be found in—

    A a food magazine

    B a restaurant guide

    C a farmer's journal

    D a physical fitness magazine

3 You can conclude from the passage that—

    A producing tasty olives takes about three days

    B eating untreated olives can probably kill a person

    C combining oleuropein with lye produces a deadly poison

    D understanding chemistry is important when processing olives

4 In the last paragraph, the word *submerged* means—

    A mixed

    B lost from sight

    C covered with liquid

    D sprinkled with sugar

Want to experience "wild Africa"? A walking safari is the way to do it. And there's no better place for a walking safari than in Zambia's Luangwa Valley. This 20,000 square mile preserve is one of the last real wilderness areas left in Africa.

A walking safari is truly an adventure. You carry no weapon and have only your own feet to get you out of danger. An armed ranger of the Zambian Wildlife Authority goes along, and stays within sight of your guide. But he can't always protect you from an angry elephant or a hungry lion. But for travelers who want to meet wildlife on its own terms, there is no more exciting experience. You can get close enough to watch a herd of hippos cooling themselves in the Luangwa River—or a herd of crocodiles feasting on a hippo. In less heart-stopping moments, you might spot a family of giraffe on a stately walk through the tall grass, or a flock of bright red bee-eaters perched in a tree.

1 You can conclude that on *most* African wildlife safaris today, people travel—

    A on foot   **B** by bicycle   **C** on elephants   **D** in motor vehicles

2 A bee-eater is a type of—

    A bird   **B** insect   **C** monkey   **D** antelope

The Girl Who Used Her Wits

a Chinese folktale

A *domineering* old woman named Fow Chow lived with her two sons and their wives, Lotus Blossom and Moon Flower. Both young women loved their husbands, but they were homesick for their village. Every day they asked their mother-in-law for permission to go home for a visit.

Eventually, Fow Chow grew tired of their pleas. "Yes, you may visit your village," the old woman said. "But you must bring back the two things I most desire in the world, or you will never see your husbands again."

"We will bring you whatever you like," the girls cried excitedly.

"Very well," said Fow Chow. "Lotus Blossom, you will bring me fire wrapped in paper. Moon Flower, you will bring me wind in paper."

The girls promised to do as Fow Chow asked, though they had no idea where they would find such strange gifts. ·

Lotus Blossom and Moon Flower had a wonderful visit in their village. But when it was time to return home, they knew they had not found the strange gifts Fow Chow had asked for, and they both began to weep.

As they sat by the side of the road, a peasant girl came along. "Why are you crying?" she asked.

The two girls described their problem to the peasant girl. "Weeping will solve nothing," she said. "You must use your wits. Come home with me, and we will find a solution."

Lotus Blossom and Moon Flower accepted the girl's invitation. As they sat on the porch of her house, it grew dark. Their new friend went inside and returned with a candle wrapped in a paper lantern.

"How wonderful!" Lotus Blossom said as she took the lantern. "Fire wrapped in paper!"

Moon Flower still could not discover how to capture wind in paper, but as the night was warm, she began to fan her face with her hand.

"That's it!" the peasant girl exclaimed. She ran into the house and returned with a paper fan.

"Wind in paper!" cried Moon Flower. "Now we can return home!"

Fow Chow was amazed to see her daughters-in-law coming up the road. "Have you disobedient girls returned without the gifts I asked for?" she demanded.

"We have done as you have asked," Lotus Blossom said. She held up her paper lantern, while Moon Flower waved her fan.

"I see *someone* has done some thinking!" said Fow Chow. "Welcome home."

1 In paragraph 1, the word *domineering* means—

A wise   **B** bossy   **C** foolish   **D** complaining

2 Who was the girl who used her wits?

A Fow Chow

B Lotus Blossom

C Moon Flower

D the peasant girl

3 With which of these statements would Fow Chow *most likely* agree?

A It is better to give than to receive.

B A mind is a terrible thing to waste.

C True love can conquer all problems.

D A picture is worth a thousand words.

4 At the end of the story, Fow Chow is—

A pleased   **B** hateful   **C** surprised   **D** disappointed

---

Where did people first use paper money? Over the centuries, money has taken many different forms, including shells, beads, rice, and elephant tusks. Gold and silver were being used as money by 2500 B.C. The first coins first appeared about 1,900 years later. But there could be no paper money until paper was invented. That happened in China, around 2,000 years ago.

The Chinese used paper for writing, drawing, and decorating walls. A special kind of paper was used to make windows. Some time around the year 800, an emperor began using official pieces of paper to pay for government purchases. It could be exchanged for gold or silver at his capital. Merchants called it "flying cash."

Real paper money came along about 200 years later. Bills were printed in red and black ink. Soon afterward, crooks began copying them and passing the fake money

off as real. The emperor's government put complicated designs on the bills to stop the *counterfeiters*. Stopping counterfeiters remains a problem with paper money to this day.

1 In paragraph 3, the word *counterfeiters* means—

A people who are angry

B people who help others

C people who need money

D people who make fake money

2 "Flying cash" was *most* like today's—

   A checks   **B** paper money   **C** credit cards   **D** stock market

3 Real paper money as described in the article could *not* have been used until the invention of—

   A printing   **B** banking   **C** computers   **D** electric power

4 Why would people prefer paper to metal money?

_____

_____

April

by Sara Teasdale

The roofs are shining from the rain,
    The sparrows twitter as they fly,
And with a windy April grace
    The little clouds go by.

Yet the back-yards are bare and brown
    With only one unchanging tree—
I could not be so sure of Spring
    Save that it sings in me.

1 How does the speaker in the poem know it's spring?

_____

_____

2 How does the poem show that April belongs to two seasons?

_____

_____

_____

_____

When a director shoots a movie, she rarely films all the scenes in the order that they appear. Instead, she will typically shoot all the scenes in one location before moving to the next, even if they include the first and last scenes in the movie. If an actor is available for only a short time, all his scenes may be filmed as a group. Directors also shoot each scene several times. Different *takes* may be shot from different angles, to show each person's reaction. Sometimes a take is spoiled by an actor's mistake, or just doesn't look right to the director. Later, an editor decides what takes to use and puts the scenes in the correct order.

1 As used in this article, the word *takes* means—

A scenes in a movie

B mistakes made by actors

C separate filmings of a scene

D money earned from ticket sales

2 Editing a movie involves—

A supervising the filming

B making changes in a script

C correcting actors' mistakes

D choosing and sequencing shots

At the end of a movie, there is a list of credits. It gives the names of the actors and what parts they played. But it also gives the names and jobs of the many people that work "behind the scenes." You've seen these job titles, and you may have wondered what they mean. The *gaffer,* for example, decides how a scene should be lit. He chooses where the lights should be placed and how intense they should be. The person who puts the lights in place is called the *best boy*—even if she's a woman. *Grips* move equipment around the set, such as the machinery used to hold and move cameras. The *boom operator* holds a microphone on a long pole so that it is near the actors but out of camera range. The *property manager* is in charge of movable items used in a scene. For a school scene, for example, she would need to find desks, books, a globe, and maps.

1 You can infer that the *key grip* on a movie crew—

A obtains keys for use in different scenes

B is in charge of moving the equipment

C is the strongest person on the set

D unlocks the set

2 For a pirate movie, the property manager would have to find—

A a ship   **B** swords   **C** an island setting   **D** colorful costumes

Shawnee Heights Neighborhood Association

A Public Meeting

will be held on Thursday, May 6 at 7:30 P.M.
in the Claiborne Middle School auditorium to discuss the following issues:

- Should the community oppose the city's plan to convert the apartment building at 700–740 Greenbrier Avenue into a homeless shelter?

- Should the community seek city matching funds for the development of a bicycle path along Tahnee Avenue from the river to Columbus Boulevard?

- Should the city install speed bumps for two blocks in each direction from Steigerwald Primary School, to be funded by local assessment?

Speakers will include
The Reverend Joseph Lowrey,
 Clerical Coalition for the Homeless
Rabbi Julius K. Peck,
 Anshei Nahal Synagogue
Karen P. Scholze,
 Shawnee Heights Homeowners League
Eugene R. Slavin,
 Shawnee Heights Merchants
 Association

Roberta Mendoza,
 Citizens for Community Involvement
Anne Sirefman,
 Certified Public Accountant
Calvin Tripp,
 Chairperson, Auto Alternatives
Delia Falconer,
 Steigerwald School Parent–Teacher
 Association
Cynthia McWilliams,
 City Council Representative, District 5

Parking available in the school parking lot, 1340 Catalpa Street, and one block south at the Freehold Medical Plaza, 1600 Freehold Avenue

Refreshments courtesy of Shawnee Heights Neighborhood Association

For further details, phone 555-7465

1 You can conclude from the notice that Shawnee Heights is the name of—

  A a city

  B a small town

  C a neighborhood within a city

  D a tract of new homes under construction

Finish Line Comprehension Skills

2 Which of these can you conclude from the notice?

    A The city is trying to make a deal with the owners of an apartment building on Greenbrier Avenue.

    B The city has already decided to turn the apartment building into a homeless shelter.

    C The apartment building has already been converted into a homeless shelter.

    D The city is trying to decide where to build a homeless shelter.

3 You can infer that some people want the speed bumps because—

    A they are bothered by traffic noise near the school

    B they want the city to repair potholes near the school

    C they want people to ride bicycles instead of driving cars

    D they are concerned that people drive too fast near the school

4 Which of the speakers is *most likely* to speak in favor of the homeless shelter?

    A Delia Falconer

    B Joseph Lowrey

    C Karen P. Scholze

    D Eugene R. Slavin

5 Which of the speakers is *most likely* to speak in favor of the bike path?

    A Roberta Mendoza

    B Julius K. Peck

    C Anne Sirefman

    D Calvin Tripp

In science, calories are a unit for measuring heat. More familiarly, though, they are a way of measuring the energy you get from food. If the calorie value you get from food exactly balances the calories your body burns, your weight remains stable. If you weigh 150 pounds, you burn 80 calories an hour even when you're lying down. Sitting up burns an additional 20 calories, and when you're standing, you burn 140 calories per hour. Walking slowly for an hour uses up 240 calories, but walking fast raises that number to 300. Swimming fast can consume 500 calories, as can playing basketball. Running burns the most calories—about 1,000 per hour.

1 You can conclude from the article that—

   A you don't use calories while you're sleeping

   B the more active you are, the more calories you use

   C if you burn more calories than you take in, you gain weight

   D older people generally use more calories than younger people

2 A scientist regards energy from food as *most* similar to—

   A heat   **B** weight   **C** motion   **D** distance

It doesn't happen very often, but unfortunately it happens *too* often: An oil tanker breaks up at sea in a storm, or hits a rock. Thousands of gallons of crude oil spill out. Any oil spill, even a small one, harms and often kills *marine* plants and animals. When fish are coated with oil, their sense of smell is damaged. Sea otters lick their fur to keep clean. If their fur is covered with oil, it poisons them. Sea birds become so coated with oil that they cannot fly. And oil seeps into clams and other shellfish, poisoning them and the animals that eat them.

Oil spills affect people, too. Beaches are ruined, and fishing becomes harder. Eventually, the movements of the waves, the heat of the sun, and human intervention clean up most oil spills. But for the largest spills, the clean-up may take ten years or longer.

1 What does the author mean by "It doesn't happen very often, but unfortunately it happens *too* often"?

   _____

   _____

2 In paragraph 1, the word *marine* means—

   A sea   **B** baby   **C** flying   **D** fighting

Finish Line Comprehension Skills

"It's raining cats and dogs." That's an expression you've no doubt heard before. No one has ever reported an actual rain of cats and dogs, but there have been instances of other creatures falling from the sky. Thousands of snakes rained down on Memphis, Tennessee, one day in 1877. According to reports, some of them were a foot and a half long. In 1947, a Marksville, Louisiana, man found hundreds of fish outside his home after a rainstorm. And on June 12, 1954, Sylvia Mowday and her children in Birmingham, England, watched in amazement as a shower of rain mixed with frogs fell to earth.

What causes animals to fall from the sky? The best guess is that they are lifted from the water by atmospheric action. The wind carries them along until it dies down enough that gravity takes over and they drop to the ground.

1 How do people *most likely* feel when they see animals falling from the sky?

A happy
B angry
C grateful
D surprised

2 Which of the following could account for a rain of animals?

A a tornado
B a lightning storm
C choppy seas
D freezing weather

During World War II, the United States was at war with Japan. As in most wars, both sides used coded messages to transmit orders. The Americans were losing many ships because of Japanese code breakers. Many of them understood English and knew how the language could be manipulated.

Then Philip Johnson had an idea. He was a U.S. Marine who had lived among the Navajo people as a child. Why not develop a code based on the Navajo language? It was understood by few people except the Navajo themselves. An entire phrase in English could be expressed as a single word in Navajo. The tone in which it was spoken affected the meaning of the word. And in 1942, it had no written form.

Johnson asked for help from among the 3,600 Navajo serving in the armed forces. Some 400 "code talkers," as they were called, signed up. They spoke to each other in their own language, but Johnson's code gave old words new meanings. For example the Navajo word *so,* meaning "big fish," came to stand for "battleship."

The plan worked. The Japanese never broke the Navajo code. After the war, the Navajo code talkers were honored for their part in securing the victory.

1 The Navajo are—

   A a Native American people   **C** an island people of the Pacific

   B a minority people in Japan   **D** a group of code-breaking experts

2 Which of these is a conclusion about the Navajo language that can be drawn from paragraph 2?

   A Speaking it requires a good singing voice.

   B It is hard for non-Navajos to learn.

   C It uses mostly one-syllable words.

   D It has its own unique alphabet.

3 You can infer that the Navajo code talkers sent their messages—

   A by smoke signal   **C** by two-way radio

   B by carrier pigeon   **D** written down and carried by spies

---

The wandering albatross is a giant among birds. It is $4\frac{1}{2}$ feet long and has wings that measure 11 feet across. As you might guess, its wings make it a champion flier. It spends almost its entire life flying over the ocean. It only comes to land to nest and raise its young on remote, rocky islands. The wandering albatross can fly 300 miles a day. In a strong wind, it can glide for hours without using its wings. In fact, it uses more energy in take-offs, landings, and diving for food than it does in flight. When it gets too tired to fly, it rests and sleeps while floating on waves.

1 What is the *most likely* reason a wandering albatross would fly 300 miles in a day?

_____

2 What would a wandering albatross do on a day when there is no strong wind?

_____

_____

Cora's Ski Trip

As Cora watched the city recede behind her, she became increasingly excited. She was really looking forward to this ski trip. They were supposed to have gone Thanksgiving weekend, but there had been an emergency at her father's business. Now they were actually on their way. Even the weather was cooperating, as if aware of Cora's desires. It was bright and sunny, with a brisk wind to give the air just a perfect winter chill.

"Stop wriggling, Corazón," her mother *admonished* her from the front seat of the car. She knew her mother meant it when she used her full name instead of her nickname.

"I can't wait till we get there! I'm going to take snowboarding lessons this time!" Cora enthused. "I don't see how you can keep your balance with both feet stuck on one board, but Gregorio told me that it's much easier than skiing. I guess I'll find out."

"Well, it will be at least two hours before we get there, so hold your horses," her dad chuckled.

Suddenly there was a strange noise coming from the car. "What's that?" Cora and her mother both questioned.

"Let me pull over and take a look," her dad said.

Mr. Andujar parked the car on the side of the road. Steam rose as he raised the hood. Moments later he appeared at the window.

"It's the radiator," he said heavily. "It's broken, and the engine is overheating. We can't risk driving the car into the mountains. We'll have to have it towed to a garage."

"Oh, no!" Cora cried. "How long will that take?" Her mother too voiced her dismay.

Mr. Andujar sighed. "I'll see," he said. He called the information number on his cell phone and asked for the number of a local garage. As Mr. Andujar explained the problem to the garage, Cora wrung her

hands and waited tensely. Then her father hung up and announced, "The garage is sending a tow truck, but it's Saturday, and there isn't a mechanic on duty to fix it until Monday."

Cora waited dejectedly for the tow truck. Nobody spoke. *The trip is ruined,* Cora thought, though she wouldn't say it out loud. *Again.*

It took about an hour for the tow truck to arrive, though Cora was no longer in any hurry. The driver got out and spoke briefly with her father. Then he asked Mr. Andujar to start the engine. He disappeared behind the raised hood as he peered into the workings of the car. Then he reappeared, smiling, and waved at Mr. Andujar to shut it off.

"It's not your radiator, it's the thermostat," he said. "I have a spare down at the garage. Once the engine cools down, I can have you back on the road in half an hour."

"Hooray!" Cora yelled, while her mother looked relieved. "Our ski trip is on!"

1 Which of these *best* describes Cora?

    A She was excited about going skiing.

    B She was timid about trying new things.

    C She was impatient when the car broke down.

    D She was embarrassed about being with her parents.

2 In paragraph 2, what does the word *admonished* mean?

    A laughed   **B** scolded   **C** explained   **D** understood

3 What will *most likely* happen next?

    A The vacation will be ruined.

    B The family will make new vacation plans.

    C The mechanic will be unable to repair the car.

    D The family will be late in arriving at the ski resort.

4 In paragraph 11, why won't Cora speak her thoughts out loud?

_____

_____

One of the strangest creatures in the sea is the Portuguese Man-of-War. Resting on top of the water is an air-filled float that is about eight to twelve inches long. Long, blue, ribbon-like tentacles hang down from the float. Though it looks like a single animal, it's actually a colony of small animals called polyps. Different polyps do different jobs to keep the colony alive. Some find food. Others lay and care for eggs. And still others fight off enemies with their stings. Although beautiful to look at, the Portuguese Man-of-War is dangerous. Its 30-foot-long tentacles contain hundreds of stinging cells. They can paralyze other sea creatures and be extremely painful and even deadly to human swimmers.

1 A Portuguese Man-of-War *most* resembles a—

    A lobster   **B** dolphin   **C** scorpion   **D** jellyfish

2 The polyps that make up a Portuguese Man-of-War form a colony that is *most* similar to a group of—

    A ants   **B** bats   **C** crows   **D** tropical fish

The youngster observed the artist at work in the park and saw a painting take form before his eyes. From that moment, Henry Ossawa Tanner was determined to be an artist, too. The year was 1872, and 13-year-old Henry, a minister's son, had no idea how difficult it was to become a painter, especially for an African American. Most collectors wanted the work of European artists. Few were interested in the work of an unknown black man.

Henry Tanner studied hard, however. He sketched the people and scenes that he saw every day in Philadephia, Pennsylvania. Later he attended art school, where he became a student of the famous artist Thomas Eakins. As an adult, he taught at Clark University in Atlanta, Georgia, while continuing to study and paint.

During the 1890s, many American artists studied in Europe. To earn money for a trip to Rome, Henry collected his best works for a one-man show. These early works show an honest and real feeling for the life of African Americans in the South. A famous picture from this period, *The Banjo Lesson,* shows a little boy sitting on an old man's lap. The man is teaching the child to play the banjo, and the love between the two shines through the painting. Although none of Henry's paintings sold at the show, some interested people later recognized his talent and decided to help him by buying his entire collection.

On his way to Rome, Henry stopped in Paris. It appealed to him so much that he couldn't leave. Paris, the City of Light, was Europe's art capital. For Henry, it was the ideal place to work and to study. He enjoyed the freedom from racism that he found there, and the friendliness of the French people. Henry now worked mostly on religious paintings, drawn from events in the Bible.

During his five years in Paris, Henry Tanner developed the style that made him famous. His colors were warm and rich, with sharp differences between light and dark areas. In 1897, the French government bought one of his paintings, *The Resurrection of Lazarus.* After that, he won many honors and prizes in both Europe and the United States before his death in 1937. Today Henry Ossawa Tanner's paintings hang in museums and galleries around the world.

1 Henry Ossawa Tanner could *best* be described as—

A sloppy and lazy

C ambitious and greedy

B sentimental and sad

D steadfast and determined

2 The Paris years were important to Tanner because—

A he developed the painting style that brought him fame

B he became America's best-loved painter there

C Paris was Europe's art capital

D he could live cheaply there

3 What influence might being a minister's son have had on Tanner's art?

_____

_____

4 According to the article, which event *most* contributed to Tanner's fame and recognition?

A He painted *The Banjo Lesson*.

B He studied with Thomas Eakins.

C The French government bought *The Resurrection of Lazarus*.

D A collector bought his paintings following his one-man show.

In the 1860s, a railroad was built across the United States that linked our country from coast to coast. It was actually two railroads, with the Union Pacific advancing from the east and the Central Pacific from the west. Most of the work was done with hand tools. The workers on the Union Pacific had it relatively easy. They were mostly laying track across the Great Plains. But the Central Pacific had to cross the high and rugged Sierra Nevada mountains of California. This work involved digging through walls of solid granite. The rock was so hard in some places that teams of strong men could only dig seven or eight inches of tunnel in a day. Explosives were used to blast through rock, but this work caused many injuries and deaths. It took more than four years for the Central Pacific to blast its line through California to the Nevada Border. The two railroads finally linked up in Utah on May 10, 1869. The transcontinental railroad cut travel time across the United States from weeks to days, but at the cost of hundreds of lives.

Finish Line Comprehension Skills

1 The hand tools referred to in the article *most likely* included—

    A hammers, screwdrivers, and tape measures

    B picks, shovels, and heavy hammers

    C axes, chain saws, and cables

    D rakes, spades, and hoes

2 The author *mainly* wants readers to know that building the Central Pacific—

    A helped unite the country

    B was bad for the environment

    C was difficult and dangerous work

    D was a good job for poorly educated workers

3 Use this chart to show evidence for your conclusion. Write your answer to question 2 under **Conclusion.** Then, under **Proof,** write three details that back up your conclusion.

Conclusion	Proof
	1. _____ _____ 2. _____ _____ 3. _____ _____

Sherlock Holmes, the most famous detective in fiction, is best known for his ability to make inferences based on the clues he finds. He first appeared in 1887, in the novel A Study in Scarlet. *His author, Arthur Conan Doyle, wrote three more novels and 56 short stories featuring Holmes and his friend, Dr. Watson, who narrates the tales. Read an adaptation of one of these stories and answer the questions after each part.*

The Adventure of the Three Students—Part 1

adapted from a story by Arthur Conan Doyle

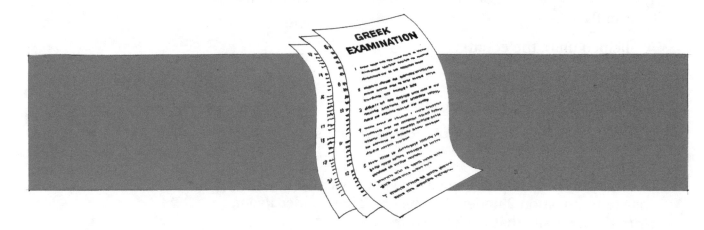

One evening Mr. Hilton Soames, a teacher at the College of St. Luke's, came to call on Sherlock Holmes.

"I trust, Mr. Holmes, that you can spare me a few hours of your time," our visitor said. "I must explain to you, Mr. Holmes, that tomorrow is the first day of the examination for the Fortescue Scholarship. I am one of the examiners. My subject is Greek, and the first of the exams consists of a long passage written in Greek that the students have not seen. The passage is printed on the examination paper, and it would naturally be an advantage if the students could prepare it in advance. For this reason, great care is taken to keep the paper secret.

"Today, about three o'clock, the exam papers arrived from the printers. I had, however, promised to visit a friend, so I left the exam on my desk. I was absent rather more than an hour. As I approached my outer door, I was amazed to see a key in it. For an instant I imagined that I had left my own there, but on feeling in my pocket I found that it was all right. The only duplicate which existed, so far as I knew, belonged to my servant, Bannister—a man who has looked after my room for ten years, and whose honesty is absolutely above suspicion. I found that the key was indeed his, that he had entered my room to know if I wanted tea, and that he had very carelessly left the key in the door when he came out.

"The moment I looked at my table, I was aware that someone had gone through my papers. The exam was in three long sheets. I had left them all together. Now I found that one of them was lying on the floor, one was on the side table near the window, and the third was where I had left it.

"For an instant I imagined that Bannister had taken the liberty of examining my papers. He denied it, however, and I am convinced that he was speaking the truth. The only other thing that could have happened was that someone passing had observed the key in the door, had known that I was out, and had entered to look at the papers. A large sum of money is at stake, because the scholarship is very valuable.

"Bannister was very much upset by the incident. He had nearly fainted when we found that the papers had been tampered with. He sat in a chair, while I made the most careful examination of the room. I soon saw that the intruder had left on the table by the window several shreds from a pencil that had been sharpened. A broken tip of lead was lying there also. Evidently the rascal had copied the paper in a great hurry, had broken his pencil, and then had to sharpen it.

"This was not all. I have a new writing table. It was smooth and unstained. Now I found a clean cut in it about three inches long. Not only this, but on the table I found a small black ball of dough or clay, with specks of something that looks like sawdust in it. I am convinced that these marks were left by the man who went through the papers. There were no footprints and no other evidence as to his identity. I was at my wit's end, when suddenly the happy thought occurred to me that you were in the town, and I came straight round to put the matter into your hands. Do help me, Mr. Holmes. You see my problem. Either I must find the man, or else the examination must be postponed until fresh papers are prepared. Since this cannot be done without an explanation, it will make the college look bad."

1 What is the crime Holmes is investigating in this story?

    A faking an ancient manuscript

    B damaging school property

    C stealing official papers

    D cheating on a test

2 Which word *best* describes Mr. Soames in this passage?

    A sad   **B** angry   **C** worried   **D** forgetful

3 Why is Soames particularly concerned about the crime?

    A The intruder damaged his room.

    B A large sum of money is involved.

    C People might mistrust his honesty.

    D Greek is a main subject at the college.

Making Inferences

4 Why is the ball of clay described in paragraph 7 important?

_____

_____

5 Predict what will happen in the next part of the story.

_____

_____

The Adventure of the Three Students—Part 2

"I shall be happy to look into it and give you such advice as I can," said Holmes. "Had anyone visited you in your room after the papers came to you?"

"Yes, young Daulet Ras, a student, came in to ask me some questions about the examination."

"For which he was entered?"

"Yes."

"And the papers were on your table?"

"To the best of my belief, they were rolled up."

"But might be recognized as the examination?"

"Possibly."

"No one else was in your room?"

"No."

"Did anyone know that the exam papers would be there?"

"No one save the printer."

"Then it amounts to this, Mr. Soames: that, unless Daulet Ras recognized the roll as test papers, the man who tampered with them came upon them accidentally without knowing that they were there."

"So it seems to me."

"Well," said Holmes, "let's go round and have a look."

The sitting-room of our client opened by a long, low window onto the courtyard of the old college. A large door led to a worn stone staircase. The teacher's room was on the ground floor. Above were three students' rooms, one on each story. Holmes halted and looked carefully at the window. Then he approached it, and, standing on tiptoe with his neck _craned,_ he looked into the room.

"He must have entered through the door. There is no opening except the one pane," said the teacher. He unlocked his outer door and ushered us into his room.

We stood at the entrance while Holmes made an examination of the carpet. "I'm afraid there are no signs here," said he. "One could hardly hope for any on so dry a day. Your servant seems to have quite recovered. You left him in a chair, you say. Which chair?"

"By the window there."

"I see. Near this little table. Let us take the little table first. What has happened is very clear. The man entered and took the papers, sheet by sheet, from the central table. He carried them over to the window table because from there he could see if you came across the courtyard, and so could escape."

"As a matter of fact, he could not," said Soames, "for I entered by the side door,"

"Ah, that's good! Well, anyhow, that was in his mind. Let me see the three sheets. No finger marks! Well, he carried over this one

Finish Line Comprehension Skills

© The Continental Press, Inc.   Do not duplicate.

first, and he copied it. Then he tossed it down and seized the next. He was in the midst of that when your return caused him to make a very hurried retreat—very hurried, since he had not time to replace the papers which would tell you he had been there. You were not aware of any hurrying feet on the stair as you entered the outer door?"

"No, I can't say I was."

"Well, he wrote so furiously that he broke his pencil, and had, as you observe, to sharpen it again. This is of interest, Watson. The pencil was not an ordinary one. It was above the usual size, with a soft lead, the outer color was dark blue, the maker's name was printed in silver lettering, and the piece remaining is only an inch and a half long. Look for such a pencil, Mr. Soames, and you have got your man. When I add that he possesses a large and very blunt knife, you have an additional aid."

1 How does Holmes conclude that the intruder came in by the door?

_____

_____

2 In paragraph 16, what does the word *craned* mean?

   A bent

   B hurting

   C stretched out

   D turned sideways

3 What signs was Holmes looking for in the carpet?

_____

4 In the last paragraph, what was Holmes inferring about the intruder and his knife?

   A He meant to use it as a weapon.

   B He used it to sharpen the pencil.

   C He used it to force open the door.

   D It was what made the scratch on the table.

The Adventure of the Three Students—Part 3

Mr. Soames was somewhat overwhelmed by this flood of information. "I can follow the other points," said he, "but really, in this matter of the length—"

Holmes held out a small chip with the letters *NN* and a space of clear wood after them. "You see?"

"No, I fear that even now—"

"What could this 'NN' be? It is at the end of a word. You are aware that Johann Faber is the most common maker's name. Is it not clear that there is just as much of the pencil left as usually follows the Johann?

"Now, for the central table. This small pellet is, I presume, the black, doughy mass you spoke of. As you say, there appear to be grains of sawdust in it. Dear me, this is very interesting. The cut on the table began with a thin scratch and ended in a jagged hole. Where does that door lead to?"

"To my bedroom."

"Have you been in it since your adventure?"

"No, I came straight away for you."

"I should like to have a glance round."

Suddenly Holmes stooped over and picked up a small pyramid of black, putty-like stuff, exactly like the one on the table of the study. "Your visitor seems to have left traces in your bedroom as well as in your sitting-room, Mr. Soames."

"What could he have wanted there?"

"I think it is clear enough. You came back by an unexpected way, and so he had no warning until you were at the very door. What could he do? He caught up everything which would give him away, and he rushed into your bedroom to hide himself."

"Good gracious, Mr. Holmes, do you mean to tell me that all the time I was talking to Bannister in this room, we had the man prisoner if we had only known it?"

"So I read it," Holmes replied. Then he asked, "Is it true that there are three students who use this stair, and are in the habit of passing your door?"

"Yes, there are."

"And they are all in for this examination?"

"Yes."

"Have you any reason to suspect any one of them more than the others?"

Soames hesitated. "It is a very hard question," said he. "One hardly likes to throw suspicion where there are no proofs."

"Let us hear the suspicions. I will look after the proofs."

Finish Line Comprehension Skills

"I will tell you, then, in a few words, the character of the three men who live in these rooms. The lower of the three is Gilchrist, a fine scholar and athletic. He got a medal winning the hurdles and the long jump. His father was the Sir Jabez Gilchrist who lost all his money gambling. Gilchrist has been left very poor, but he is hardworking.

"The second floor is inhabited by Daulat Ras. He is a quiet fellow. He is well up in his work, though Greek is his weak subject.

"The top floor belongs to Miles McLaren. He is a brilliant fellow when he chooses to work, but he is lazy."

"Then it is he whom you suspect?"

"I dare not go as far as that."

"Now, Mr. Soames, let us have a look at your servant, Bannister."

1 How did Holmes determine that the guilty student had a short pencil?

_____

_____

2 How did Holmes infer that the guilty student hid in the bedroom?

_____

_____

3 What was the athletic student Gilchrist's sport?

A   soccer

B   swimming

C   horsemanship

D   track and field

4 What reason did Holmes have to suspect each of the three students?

a.   Gilchrist _____

b.   Ras _____

c.   McLaren _____

The Adventure of the Three Students—Part 4

Bannister was a little, gray-haired fellow of fifty.

"We are investigating this unhappy business, Bannister," said the teacher.

"Yes, sir."

"I understand," said Holmes, "that you left your key in the door?"

"Yes, sir."

"Was it not very *extraordinary* that you should do this on the very day when there were these papers inside?"

"It was most unfortunate, sir. But I have occasionally done the same thing at other times."

"When did you enter the room?"

"It was about half past four. That is Mr. Soames's tea time."

"How long did you stay?"

"When I saw that he was absent, I left at once."

"Did you look at these papers on the table?"

"No, sir, certainly not."

"How came you to leave the key in the door?"

"I had the tea-tray in my hand. I thought I would come back for the key. Then I forgot."

"When Mr. Soames returned and called for you, you were very much disturbed?"

"Yes, sir. Such a thing has never happened during the many years that I have been here. I nearly fainted, sir."

"Where were you when you began to feel bad?"

"Why, here, near the door."

"That is strange, because you sat down in that chair over yonder near the corner. Why did you pass these other chairs?"

"I don't know, sir, it didn't matter to me where I sat."

"You stayed here when the teacher left?"

"Only for a minute or so. Then I locked the door and went to my room."

"Thank you, that will do," said Holmes. "Very good. Now, Mr. Soames, we will take a walk in the courtyard, if you please."

Three yellow squares of light shone above us in the gathering gloom.

"Your three birds are all in their nests," said Holmes, looking up. "I should like to have a peep at each of them. Is it possible?"

"No difficulty in the world," Soames answered.

"No names, please!" said Holmes, as we knocked at Gilchrist's door.

Finish Line Comprehension Skills

A tall, yellow-haired, slim young fellow opened it, and made us welcome when he understood our errand. There were some really curious pieces of woodwork within. Holmes was so charmed with one of them that he insisted on drawing it in his notebook, broke his pencil, and had to borrow one from our host, and finally borrowed a knife to sharpen it. The same curious accident happened to him in the rooms of Daulat Ras, who was short and thin. I could not see that in either case Holmes had come upon the clue for which he was searching.

At the third door we were greeted with shouting. "I don't care who you are!" roared the angry voice. "Tomorrow's the exam, and I won't be disturbed by anyone."

"A rude fellow," said our guide, flushing with anger as we withdrew down the stair. "Of course he did not realize that it was I who was knocking, but nonetheless his conduct was most *discourteous,* and indeed, under the circumstances, rather suspicious."

Holmes's response was a curious one. "Can you tell me his exact height?" he asked.

"Really, Mr. Holmes, I cannot undertake to say. He is taller than Daulat Ras, not so tall as Gilchrist. I suppose five foot six would be about it."

"That is very important," said Holmes. "And now, sir, I wish you good-night."

Soames cried aloud in his astonishment. "Good gracious, Mr. Holmes, you are surely not going to leave! You don't seem to realize the position I am in. Tomorrow is the examination. I must take some action tonight. I cannot allow the examination to be held if one of the papers has been tampered with."

"You must leave it as it is. I shall drop round early tomorrow morning and chat the matter over. It is possible that I may be in a position then to indicate some course of action. Meanwhile, you change nothing— nothing at all."

"Very good, Mr. Holmes."

1 Why did Holmes ask Gilchrist and Ras if he could borrow a pencil and a knife?

_____

_____

2 What does the word *extraordinary* mean in paragraph 6?

  A foolish   **B** unlucky   **C** surprising   **D** not truthful

3 What does the word *discourteous* mean in paragraph 31?

  A rude   **B** nervous   **C** painful   **D** terrifying

4 Who do you think is guilty? Explain why.

_____

_____

_____

The Adventure of the Three Students—Part 5

At eight in the morning, Holmes came into my room. "Well, Watson," said he, "it is time we went down to St. Luke's."

"Have you anything positive to tell Soames?"

"Yes, my dear Watson, I have solved the mystery."

"But what fresh evidence could you have got?"

"Aha! It is not for nothing that I have turned myself out of bed at the *untimely* hour of six! I have put in two hours' hard work and covered at least five miles, with something to show for it. Look at that!" He held out his hand. On the palm were three little pyramids of black, doughy clay. "Why, Holmes, you only had two yesterday!"

"And one more this morning. It is a fair argument that wherever No. 3 came from is also the source of Nos. 1 and 2. Eh, Watson? Well, come along and put friend Soames out of his pain."

The unfortunate teacher was quite worried. "Thank heaven that you have come! I feared that you had given it up. What am I to do? Shall the examination proceed?"

"Yes, let it proceed, by all means."

"But this rascal?"

"He shall not take the exam."

"You know him?"

"I think so. If this matter is not to become public, we must hold a meeting. Kindly ring for Bannister."

Bannister entered, looking fearful.

"You will kindly close the door," said Holmes. "Now, Bannister, will you please tell us the truth about yesterday's incident."

"I have told you everything, sir."

"Nothing to add?"

"Nothing at all, sir."

"Well, then, I must make some suggestions to you. When you sat down on the chair yesterday, did you do so in order to conceal some object which would have shown who had been in the room?"

Bannister's face was ghastly.

"It is only a suggestion," said Holmes. "I frankly admit that I am unable to prove it. But it seems probable enough since the moment that Mr. Soames's back was turned, you released the man who was hiding in that bedroom."

Bannister licked his dry lips. "There was no man, sir."

"Ah, that's a pity, Bannister. Up to now, you may have spoken the truth, but now I know that you have lied."

"There was no man, sir."

"Come, come, Bannister."

Finish Line Comprehension Skills

"No, sir, there was no one."

"In that case, you can give us no further information. Would you please remain in the room? Stand over there near the bedroom door. Now, Soames, I am going to ask you to have the great kindness to go up to the room of young Gilchrist and to ask him to step down into yours."

An instant later the teacher returned, bringing with him the student. His troubled blue eyes glanced at each of us.

"Just close the door," said Holmes. "Now, Mr. Gilchrist, we are all quite alone here, and no one need ever know one word of what passes between us. We can be perfectly frank with each other. We want to know, Mr. Gilchrist, how you, an honorable man, ever came to commit such an action as that of yesterday."

The unfortunate young man staggered back and cast a look of full horror at Bannister.

"No, no, Mr. Gilchrist, sir, I never said a word—never one word!" cried the servant.

"No, but you have now," said Holmes. "Now, sir, you must see that after Bannister's words your position is hopeless, and that your only chance lies in a frank confession."

For a moment Gilchrist, with upraised hand, tried to control his expression. The next he had thrown himself on his knees beside the table, and burying his face in his hands, he had burst into a storm of sorrowful sobbing.

"Come, come," said Holmes, kindly, "it is human to err, and at least no one can accuse you of being a hardened criminal. Perhaps it would be easier for you if I were to tell Mr. Soames what occurred, and you can check me where I am wrong? Shall I do so? Well, well, don't trouble to answer. Listen, and see that I do you no injustice."

1 What does the word *untimely* mean in paragraph 5?

   A too late

   B just in time

   C at a bad time

   D not caring about time

2 What fact led Holmes to suspect Gilchrist?

   _____

   _____

3 Why did Holmes ask Bannister to stay in the room while he questioned Gilchrist?

   _____

   _____

4 What did Bannister do that indicated Gilchrist was guilty?

   _____

   _____

Making Inferences

The Adventure of the Three Students—Part 6

"From the moment, Mr. Soames, that you said to me that no one, not even Bannister, knew that the papers were in your room, the case began to take a definite shape in my mind. Daulat Ras I thought nothing of. If the exam papers were in a roll, he could not possibly know what they were. On the other hand, it seemed an unthinkable coincidence that a man should dare to enter the room, and that by chance on that very day the papers were on the table. I dismissed that. The man who entered knew that the papers were there. How did he know?

"When I approached your room, I examined the window. I was measuring how tall a man would need to be in order to see, as he passed, what papers were on the central table. I am six feet high, and I could do it with effort. No one less than that would have chance. Already you see I had reason to think that, if one of your three students was a man of unusual height, he was the most worth watching of the three.

"I entered, and I took you into my confidence as to the suggestions of the side table. Of the center table I could make nothing, until in your description of Gilchrist you mentioned that he was a long-jumper. Then the whole thing came to me in an instant, and I only needed certain proofs, which I speedily obtained.

"What happened was this: This young fellow had spent the afternoon at the athletic grounds, where he had been practicing the jump. He returned carrying his jumping-shoes, which are provided, as you know, with several sharp spikes. As he passed your window he saw, by means of his great height, these papers upon your table, and guessed what they were. No harm would have been done had it not been that, as he passed your door, he saw the key which had been left by the carelessness of your servant. A sudden impulse came over him to enter and see if they were indeed the exam papers. It was not a dangerous deed, for he could always pretend that he had simply looked in to ask a question.

"Well, when he saw that they were indeed the exam papers, it was then that he yielded to temptation. He put his shoes on the table. What was it that you put on that chair near the window?"

"Gloves," said the young man.

Finish Line Comprehension Skills

"He put his gloves on the chair, and he took the exam papers, sheet by sheet, to copy them. He thought the teacher must return by the main gate, and that he would see him. As we know, he came back by the side gate. Suddenly he heard him at the very door. There was no possible escape. He forgot his gloves, but he caught up his shoes and darted into the bedroom. You observe the scratch on that table is slight at one side but deepens in the direction of the bedroom door. That in itself is enough to show us that the shoe had been drawn in that direction, and that the *culprit* had gone in there. The earth round the spike had been left on the table, and a second sample was loosened and fell in the bedroom. I may add that I walked out to the athletic grounds this morning, saw that black clay is used in the jumping-pit, and carried away a piece of it, together with the fine tan of sawdust which is strewn over it to prevent the athlete from slipping. Have I told the truth, Mr. Gilchrist?"

The student had drawn himself erect. "Yes, sir, it is true," said he.

1 What did the evidence that Holmes picked up that morning prove?

  A The mounds of clay in Soames's apartment had come from the athletic field.

  B The scratch on Soames's table had been made by Gilchrist's shoe.

  C Only Gilchrist could have coped the exam papers.

  D Bannister had helped Gilchrist copy the exam.

2 Why had Bannister chosen to sit on the chair near the window?

_____

3 What does the word *culprit* mean in paragraph 7?

  A shoe   **B** athlete   **C** piece of dirt   **D** guilty person

4 Predict what will happen in the last part of the story.

_____

_____

_____

The Adventure of the Three Students—Part 7

"Good heavens! Have you nothing to add?" cried Soames.

"Yes, sir, I have. I have a letter here, Mr. Soames, which I wrote to you early this morning after a restless night. It was before I knew that my sin had found me out. Here it is, sir. You will see that I have said, 'I have determined not to go in for the examination. I have been offered a job overseas in the police, and I am going at once.'"

"I am indeed pleased to hear that you did not intend to profit by your unfair advantage," said Soames. "But why did you change your purpose?"

Gilchrist pointed to Bannister. "There is the man who set me in the right path," said he.

"Come now, Bannister," said Holmes, "It will be clear from what I have said, that only you could have let this young man out, since you were left in the room and must have locked the door when you went out. Can you not clear up the last point in this mystery and tell us the reasons for your action?"

"It was simple enough, sir, if only you had known," said the servant, "but with all your cleverness, it was impossible that you could know. Time was, sir, when I was butler to old Sir Jabez Gilchrist, this young gentleman's father. When he lost his money, I came to the college as a servant, but I never forgot my old employer because he was down in the world. I watched his son all I could for the sake of the old days. Well, sir, when I came into this room yesterday, the first thing I saw was Mr. Gilchrist's tan gloves a-lying in that chair. I knew those gloves well, and I understood their message. If Mr. Soames saw them, the game was up. I flopped down into that chair, and nothing would budge me until Mr. Soames went for you. Then out came my poor young man and confessed it all to me. Wasn't it natural, sir, that I should save him, and wasn't it natural also that I should try to speak to him as his dead father would have done, and make him understand that he could not profit by such a deed? Could you blame me, sir?"

"No, indeed," said Holmes heartily, springing to his feet. "Well, Soames, I think we have cleared your little problem up, and our breakfast awaits us at home. Come, Watson! As to you, sir, I trust that a bright future awaits you in your new job. For once you have fallen low. Let us see, in the future, how high you can rise."

1 Why did Bannister try to help Gilchrist?

_____

_____

2 What do you think will happen to Gilchrist in the future? Explain why.

_____

_____

_____

_____